DRS. ING. PASCAL HUIJBERS

Smart Machines, Smart Choices

The Executive's Guide to Navigating Quantum and AI

Thanks for being Healthy, thanks for being Smart, Thanks for my lovely kids and my beautiful partner. Thanks for the Sea and the Wind.

Contents

Foreword

In the last 20 years i have often written and presented on the impact of emerging technologies and how they will impact society and business as well as people in their daily lives.

When i was a student i worked as an IT admin in my hours outside my study, well lets say i studied outside the hours that i worked :) One of my colleagues at that time was a salesperson and he started his own "real estate" broker as part of the larger very known Association of real estate Brokers in the netherlands. At that time internet was nothing more then a floppy and modem to dial in. Browsers were just coming in to use at that time. When he started his broker we discussed that we would build a website together that would reflect all the houses that were for sale and he would do this for this large association. We never build it, i thought that nobody would even go to a website like that looking for houses to buy. Little did i know since these website are now probably the most visited websites in the netherlands and is the place to look for a house.

Learning from my mistake i told myself that from now on i would jump on every upcoming trend and do something with it, either a new initiative, a publication or a company. And i did. With everything becoming smart we need to make smart choices. Welcome to the future of the Smart Machine age

Preface

Today , more than 1500 years ago, in ancient china, a wise mathematician invented the game of chess. The emperor, impressed by the invention's strategic depth and the intellectual challenge it presented, offered the inventor any reward he desired. The mathematician's request was simple but profound: he asked for a single grain of rice to be placed on the first square of the chessboard. Then, double that number for the second square, double it again for the third, and continue this way, doubling the grains for each of the 64 squares.

The emperor readily agreed, unaware of the deceptive power of exponential growth. What seemed like a humble request soon spiraled into astronomical figures, far exceeding the entire empire's rice reserves and, in fact, surpassing the world's rice production.

What's tricky about this is that for the first few squares, the growth appears linear, almost negligible. A single grain becomes two, then four, then eight, and so on. It's not until you reach the 33rd square that you begin to see the curve steepen dramatically. By the time you get to the 64th square, the numbers are incom-prehensible, edging into the realm of astronomical figures. The growth is not linear as it seemed at first, its actually exponential.

This ancient parable holds a profound lesson for our under-standing of technology's growth trajectory, particularly in the realms of Artificial Intelligence (AI) and quantum computing. For decades, we've watched technology advance at what seemed like a consistent pace. Moore's Law, the observation that the number of transistors on a microchip doubles approximately every two years, seemed to encapsulate this steady progress. However, much like the grains of rice on the chessboard, we're beginning to realize that we're not dealing with linear growth; we're facing exponential growth. And just like the emperor, we might be ill-prepared for what this means.

We are now entering what could be considered the "second half of the chessboard" in technological advancements. With developments in AI algorithms, machine learning capabilities, and quantum computing, technology is not just doubling; it is reshaping the very fabric of society at an exponential rate. The numbers, the capabilities, and the potential impact have grown so large that they are hard to comprehend—much less predict.

As we delve into this comprehensive examination of AI and quantum computing's current status and future impact, keep the lesson of the chessboard in mind. The stakes are high, and the growth is exponential. We're no longer in the realm of steady, predictable advancements. We're in a territory where each move can dramatically amplify the outcomes, for better or worse.

Chapter 1: The Impact of the Smart Machine Age

The term "Smart Machine Age" encapsulates the time we find ourselves in, characterized by unprecedented advancements in technology. Unlike any other period in human history, this era is driven by intelligent machines that can learn, adapt, and even make decisions. We've moved beyond the simple digitization of tasks to a realm where machines can analyze vast amounts of data, make complex calculations in nanoseconds, and automate decision-making processes that would take humans considerably longer.

It's crucial to differentiate the Smart Machine Age from the Information Age that preceded it. While the Information Age was defined by the ability to store, process, and transmit information in digital formats, the Smart Machine Age takes this a step further by adding layers of intelligence to this information. It's not just about having access to data anymore; it's about making that data work for you in ways that were unimaginable even a decade ago.

The Smart Machine Age is not just the product of one or two groundbreaking technologies; it's the result of a confluence of several. Artificial Intelligence (AI), Quantum Computing, Internet of Things (IoT), and Big Data, among others, are coming together in a synergistic manner. Each of these technologies is powerful in its own right, but when combined, they have the potential to transform our world in ways that are still hard to fully grasp.

The societal impacts of the Smart Machine Age are multifaceted and complex. On one hand, we have incredible advancements in healthcare, education, and public services. AI algorithms can diagnose diseases with a level of accuracy that rivals seasoned medical professionals. Educational platforms can adapt in real-time to the learning styles of individual students. However, there are also significant concerns about job displacement due to automation, data privacy, and the ethical implications of machines making decisions that have traditionally been the purview of humans.

The Smart Machine Age promises to bring about seismic shifts in the global economy. Industries that have been pillars of economic stability for decades are finding themselves disrupted by smart technologies. The financial sector, for instance, is undergoing a transformation driven by AI algorithms capable of high-frequency trading and risk assessment at speeds no human could match. Similarly, the manufacturing sector is seeing the advent of smart factories where AI-driven robots handle tasks ranging from assembly to quality control.

One of the most overlooked aspects of the Smart Machine Age is its impact on governance and public policy. As smart technologies become increasingly integrated into our daily lives, there's an urgent need for governance models that can address the unique challenges they present. This includes everything from data protection laws to regulations governing the use of AI in critical public services like healthcare and law enforcement.

While the Smart Machine Age holds immense promise, it also risks exacerbating existing inequalities. The benefits of smart technologies are not distributed evenly across society. There's a very real danger that those who are already disadvantaged will find themselves further marginalized as the world around them becomes increasingly automated and data-driven. Bridging this digital divide is one of the most pressing challenges we face as we navigate the complexities of this new epoch.

How the Smart Machine Age Differs from Previous Technological Eras

To fully appreciate the uniqueness of the Smart Machine Age, one must contextualize it within the broader sweep of technological history. The Industrial Revolution marked the first significant mechanization of labor, but it was limited to repetitive, physical tasks. The advent of the computer age expanded this to include data processing tasks, fundamentally altering industries like finance, media, and telecommunications. However, none of these previous eras had the capability to 'think' and 'learn'—a domain that was exclusively human.

The term 'quantum leap' is often used metaphorically to describe significant advancements, but in the context of the Smart Machine Age, it's quite literal. Quantum Computing, a subject we'll delve into in greater detail in Chapter 3, promises computational speeds and capabilities that are orders of magnitude greater than current technologies. This isn't just about doing things faster; it's about doing things that were previously impossible or impractical.

The defining characteristic that sets the Smart Machine Age apart from previous eras is the infusion of cognitive abilities into technology. AI algorithms can now understand, learn, and even reason to a certain extent. They can recognize patterns in data that would be invisible to human analysts, predict outcomes based on complex multi-variable analyses, and adapt to new information in real-time. In essence, we're transitioning from tools that assist human cognition to tools that possess their own form of limited cognition.

Previous technological eras have had their economic winners and losers, but the Smart Machine Age threatens to upend the economic landscape in unprecedented ways. Traditional sectors like manufacturing and agriculture are already feeling the heat from automation and smart farming techniques. Meanwhile, sectors that didn't even exist a few years ago, such as the data analytics industry, are becoming economic powerhouses. This shift has profound implications for workforce development, income distribution, and even geopolitical power dynamics.

The societal implications of the Smart Machine Age are complex and often paradoxical. On one hand, we have the democratization of information and services. Telemedicine platforms powered by AI can provide high-quality healthcare to remote or underserved areas. On the other hand, the automation of jobs, particularly low-skilled jobs, threatens to widen the gap between the haves and the have-nots. Social systems and safety nets will need to be rethought to address these new disparities.

Governance in the Smart Machine Age is entering uncharted waters. Traditional regulatory frameworks are ill-equipped to deal with the ethical, security, and equity challenges posed by smart technologies. How do you regulate an AI algorithm that learns and evolves in real-time? How do you ensure data privacy when even anonymized data can be re-identified through smart algorithms? These are questions that policymakers are just beginning to grapple with.

The ethical considerations of the Smart Machine Age are both immediate and far-reaching. Decision-making algorithms, if not carefully designed and regulated, can perpetuate existing societal biases. The use of AI in areas like judicial sentencing or loan approval brings up serious ethical concerns about fairness and accountability. Moreover, as machines take on more human-like cognitive functions, questions about the rights and ethical treatment of increasingly 'smart' machines themselves might become pertinent.

Transformative Impacts on Society, Economy, and Governance

One of the most talked-about impacts of the Smart Machine Age is on the future of work. Automation has always been viewed with a degree of trepidation, and the Smart Machine Age intensifies these concerns. Machines can now perform not just repetitive physical tasks but also complex cognitive functions like data analysis and decision-making. However, it's essential to recognize that automation also creates new job categories that didn't exist before. The challenge lies in workforce development and retraining programs that can equip people with the skills needed for the jobs of the future.

The education sector is ripe for transformation, and the Smart Machine Age brings exciting possibilities. Adaptive learning platforms, powered by AI, can tailor educational content to individual learning styles and paces. Virtual Reality (VR) can provide immersive educational experiences that are particularly beneficial for subjects like history and science, where visualization can enhance understanding. However, the integration of these technologies into educational systems raises questions about accessibility and the potential widening of educational inequality.

The role of smart technologies in shaping public opinion and democratic processes is a growing area of concern. While the Internet has democratized access to information, the rise of smart algorithms can also lead to the 'echo chamber' effect, where individuals are only exposed to information that aligns with their existing beliefs. Moreover, the misuse of AI in spreading misinformation poses significant challenges to democratic systems. Governance models need to evolve to address these unique challenges, ensuring that the benefits of smart technologies can be leveraged to strengthen rather than undermine democratic systems.

As mentioned in the previous section, the Smart Machine Age is ushering in a new economic order. Traditional economic powerhouses like the manufacturing and energy sectors are undergoing disruptive changes. AI algorithms optimize production processes, reduce waste, and improve supply chain efficiency. Quantum computing has the potential to revolutionize energy distribution and even make significant strides in the fight against climate change through more efficient materials and processes. However, this shift in economic power also brings challenges, including geopolitical tensions and the need for new economic policies and regulations.

The governance challenges of the Smart Machine Age cannot be overstated. Regulatory frameworks developed in the pre-smart machine era are woefully inadequate to address the current challenges. Issues like data privacy, algorithmic accountability, and ethical considerations require a rethinking of existing laws and regulations. Policymakers need to collaborate closely with technologists, ethicists, and other stakeholders to develop governance models that are adaptive and resilient, capable of keeping pace with rapid technological advancements.

As smart machines take on increasingly complex tasks, including decision-making that impacts human lives, ethical and moral questions become more urgent. For instance, should an autonomous vehicle prioritize the safety of its passengers over pedestrians? Who is accountable if an AI-powered healthcare platform misdiagnoses a condition? These questions don't have easy answers, but they are questions that society must address as we become increasingly reliant on smart machines.

Chapter 2: Emerging Technologies in the Smart Machine Age

A Panorama of Emerging Technologies

When people think of AI, they often visualize robots or automated customer service bots. However, AI is a multidimensional field that encompasses machine learning, natural language processing, computer vision, and robotics, among others. Machine learning algorithms are now sophisticated enough to analyze not just structured data like spreadsheets but also unstructured data like text and images. Natural language processing has reached a point where AI can understand and generate human-like text, a capability that has spawned the field of generative AI, which we will discuss in Chapter 5.

Next to AI there are other technologies that are becoming mature. On themselves these technologies already have their own use cases but in combination they really make the difference. Especially the combination of AI, Unlimited Computing power and the availability of unlimited digital data pushes us in the Smart Machine Age. Lets take a look at the relevant technologies that are coming together.

The Reality of Virtual and Augmented Reality

Virtual Reality (VR) and Augmented Reality (AR) are often considered the stuff of science fiction, but they are increasingly becoming a reality. VR immerses users in a completely digital environment, while AR overlays digital information on the real world. These technologies have applications that go far beyond gaming. In healthcare, VR can be used for everything from surgical simulation to exposure therapy for PTSD. In retail, AR apps can let customers visualize products in their real-world environment before making a purchase.

The Internet of Things: A Connected World

The Internet of Things (IoT) is another emerging technology that promises to revolutionize our daily lives. IoT refers to the network of physical objects embedded with sensors, software, and other technologies to collect and exchange data. From smart homes that adjust the thermostat based on your preferences to industrial IoT that can monitor machinery in real-time, the applications are limitless. However, IoT also raises significant concerns about data privacy and security, issues that governance models must address.

Big Data: The New Oil

In the Smart Machine Age, data is often referred to as the 'new oil.' Big Data technologies enable the collection, storage, and analysis of vast amounts of data that traditional databases cannot handle. This data can be analyzed for trends, patterns, and insights, driving decision-making in almost every sector. However, like oil, data must be refined to be valuable. This involves complex algorithms that can analyze the data and convert it into actionable insights.

Blockchain: Beyond Cryptocurrencies

Blockchain is commonly associated with cryptocurrencies like Bitcoin, but its applications are far more wide-ranging. At its core, blockchain is a decentralized, distributed ledger that can record transactions across multiple computers. This ensures that once a transaction is recorded, it cannot be altered retroactively. This has applications in sectors like supply chain management, healthcare records, and even voting systems. The decentralized nature of blockchain also presents challenges, particularly in terms of regulation and governance.

Quantum Computing: The Next Frontier

Quantum Computing is perhaps the most groundbreaking of all emerging technologies. Utilizing the principles of quantum mechanics, it promises computational speeds that are orders of magnitude faster than current technologies. This is not just about doing things faster; it's about solving complex problems that are currently unsolvable. We will delve deeper into Quantum Computing in Chapter 3.

Cybersecurity: The Invisible Shield

As we become increasingly reliant on digital technologies, the importance of cybersecurity cannot be overstated. Emerging technologies like AI and blockchain are also being employed to enhance cybersecurity measures. AI algorithms can monitor networks in real-time, detecting anomalies that could indicate a security breach. Blockchain can secure transactions and data, making it more difficult for unauthorized access.

2.2 Technological Readiness and Maturity

Artificial Intelligence is no longer an emerging technology in the conventional sense; it has matured significantly over the past decade. Especially with the recent launches of ChatGpt and other generative AI and AI models it's on everyone's mind. Yet, it continues to evolve at an exponential rate, defying the traditional life cycle of technological maturation. While machine learning algorithms have been around for years, the advent of deep learning and neural networks has catapulted AI into new domains. Today, AI is at a stage where it is not only mature but also highly adaptable, capable of learning and evolving, thereby ensuring its long-term relevance.

Quantum Computing: Nascent but Promising

Compared to AI, Quantum Computing is in its infancy, yet it holds immense promise. The technology is still in the experimental stage, with practical, scalable quantum computers yet to be built. However, advancements in quantum algorithms and error correction methods are accelerating the path to maturity. While it may take another decade or more for quantum computing to reach the level of readiness that AI currently enjoys, the technology holds the potential to revolutionize fields ranging from cryptography to material science.

Internet of Things: Bridging the Gap Between Physical and Digital

The Internet of Things (IoT) has reached a significant level of maturity, particularly in industrial applications. Smart sensors and IoT platforms are now commonplace in manufacturing, logistics, and even agriculture. However, the technology still faces challenges in terms of interoperability, security, and data management. As edge computing technologies mature, they promise to alleviate some of these challenges, pushing IoT closer to its full potential.

Big Data: Mature Yet Evolving

Big Data technologies have matured to a point where they are a staple in almost all sectors. Tools for data collection, storage, and analysis have reached high levels of sophistication. Yet, as the volume of data continues to grow, so does the technology to handle it. New algorithms and data processing frameworks are continuously being developed to handle the ever-increasing complexity and volume of data.

Virtual Reality and Augmented Reality: Beyond the Hype Cycle

VR and AR have moved beyond the 'hype cycle' and are finding practical applications. While the gaming and entertainment sectors were early adopters, industries like healthcare, real estate, and education are now leveraging these technologies. Hardware limitations, such as the bulkiness of VR headsets or the battery life of AR devices, remain challenges. However, as the hardware continues to improve, these technologies are expected to reach greater levels of maturity and adoption.

Blockchain: Navigating the Trough of Disillusionment

Blockchain technology has passed the peak of inflated expectations and is now navigating the 'trough of disillusionment,' as per Gartner's Hype Cycle. The technology has proven its value in various applications beyond cryptocurrency, but it still faces challenges in terms of scalability, energy efficiency, and regulatory acceptance. As these challenges are addressed, Blockchain is expected to reach a plateau of productivity, signifying its maturity.

Cybersecurity: An Ongoing Arms Race

Cybersecurity technology is in a constant state of flux, engaged in an ongoing 'arms race' with cybercriminals. As new security measures are developed, new types of attacks emerge, making cybersecurity a field that can never truly reach a state of complete maturity. Technologies like AI and Blockchain are being incorporated into cybersecurity solutions to enhance their effectiveness, but the evolving nature of cyber threats ensures that cybersecurity remains a continually emerging field.

2.3 Synergies: The Whole is Greater than the Sum of Its Parts

The relationship between Artificial Intelligence and Big Data is perhaps the most straightforward example of technological synergy. AI algorithms require vast amounts of data to learn, adapt, and make decisions. Big Data provides the requisite volume, variety, and velocity of data that AI needs to be effective. Conversely, the sheer amount of data generated today would be impossible to analyze without AI's data-processing capabilities. When integrated, these two technologies enable a level of data analytics and decision-making that neither could achieve on its own.

AI and IoT: Smart Decisions in Real-Time

The Internet of Things (IoT) allows for the collection of vast amounts of data from the physical world, but it is the integration of AI that enables actionable insights to be drawn from this data. For example, smart sensors on industrial machinery can detect anomalies, but it's the AI algorithms that can predict equipment failure before it happens, allowing for preventative maintenance. The synergy between AI and IoT is giving rise to intelligent ecosystems that can adapt and respond to changing conditions in real-time.

Quantum Computing and Cybersecurity: The Future of Encryption

While still in its nascent stages, Quantum Computing holds the potential to revolutionize cybersecurity. Traditional encryption methods, which are computationally intensive to break, could be easily cracked with a sufficiently advanced quantum computer. However, Quantum Computing also offers solutions, such as quantum encryption methods, that are theoretically unbreakable. The synergy between Quantum Computing and cybersecurity represents a paradigm shift in how we think about digital security.

VR and AI: Immersive, Adaptive Experiences

Virtual Reality (VR) offers immersive environments, but the integration of AI can make these environments adaptive and interactive. For example, in educational settings, an AI algorithm could monitor how a student interacts with a VR-based learning module, adapting the difficulty level or providing additional information as needed. Similarly, in healthcare, VR can be used for exposure therapy for phobias or PTSD, with AI algorithms adjusting the therapy based on the patient's physiological responses.

Blockchain and IoT: Trust in a Connected World

The decentralized nature of blockchain makes it a natural fit for IoT applications, especially in scenarios that require trust and verification. For example, in supply chain management, IoT sensors can track the location and condition of products in transit. When this data is recorded on a blockchain, it provides an immutable, verifiable record that can be trusted by all parties involved. This combination of technologies offers a level of transparency and accountability that neither could achieve independently.

Big Data and Cybersecurity: Predictive Policing of the Digital Realm

Big Data analytics have increasingly been applied to cybersecurity, allowing for predictive policing of networks. Traditional security measures are often reactive, responding to attacks after they have occurred. In contrast, Big Data analytics can analyze network behavior in real-time, identifying anomalies that could indicate a potential security threat. When combined, Big Data and cybersecurity technologies can offer a more proactive approach to digital security.

The Convergence of Technologies

Perhaps the most compelling demonstration of these synergies is in the field of smart cities. Here, AI, IoT, Big Data, and blockchain come together in a seamless integration. IoT sensors collect data on everything from traffic patterns to air quality. This data is then analyzed by AI algorithms to optimize traffic lights, adjust public transportation schedules, and even direct law enforcement resources. Blockchain ensures the security and transparency of this data, while Big Data analytics provide the tools for long-term urban planning. The smart city is a living example of how the convergence of these technologies can result in solutions far more advanced than what each could achieve individually.

Chapter 3: Unveiling Quantum Computing

The Fundamentals of Quantum Computing

Quantum Computing is often heralded as the next frontier in computation, and for a good reason. To understand its revolutionary potential, one must first appreciate the fundamental differences between quantum and classical computing. Classical computers use bits as the basic unit of information, which can either be a 0 or a 1. Quantum computers, on the other hand, use quantum bits or qubits. Unlike classical bits, qubits can exist in multiple states simultaneously, thanks to quantum phenomena like superposition and entanglement.

The Concept of Superposition

In classical computing, a bit must be either a 0 or a 1. However, a qubit in superposition can be both 0 and 1 at the same time. Imagine being able to read two different books simultaneously or navigate multiple routes at once to find the quickest way home. That's the kind of parallelism superposition offers. It allows quantum computers to perform multiple calculations in parallel, making them exponentially faster than classical computers for specific tasks.

Entanglement: A Quantum Quirk

Another fundamental concept in quantum computing is entanglement. In a classical system, the state of each bit is independent of the others. In a quantum system, qubits can become entangled, meaning the state of one qubit is intrinsically linked to another, regardless of the distance separating them. This property allows for highly complex computations to be carried out much more efficiently than in classical systems.

Quantum Gates and Circuits

In classical computing, logical operations (like AND, OR, NOT, etc.) are performed using logic gates. Quantum computing also uses gates—quantum gates—to perform operations. However, these gates operate on qubits in superposition or entanglement, allowing for a far more extensive range of operations than classical gates. Quantum circuits, made up of a sequence of quantum gates, can perform complex computations that would be practically impossible for classical circuits.

The unique properties of quantum systems have led to the development of quantum algorithms that are fundamentally different from their classical counterparts. Algorithms like Shor's algorithm for integer factorization or Grover's algorithm for unsorted database searching show that certain computational problems can be solved exponentially faster on a quantum computer.

Quantum Error Correction: The Elephant in the Room

While the theoretical potential of quantum computing is staggering, practical implementation faces significant challenges. Quantum systems are highly susceptible to errors due to environmental interference, a phenomenon known as 'quantum decoherence.' Quantum error correction techniques are in development to mitigate these issues, but they require additional qubits for error-checking, making the systems more complex.

Building a functional quantum computer is a massive engineering challenge. Quantum systems require extremely low temperatures to maintain superposition and entanglement. They also need to be isolated from all external influences, which could induce errors. Various approaches, like using trapped ions or superconducting circuits, are under exploration to build stable, scalable quantum computers.

Despite these challenges, the promise of quantum computing is too significant to ignore. From simulating complex molecular structures for drug discovery to optimizing large-scale logistical operations, the applications are endless. Moreover, quantum computing could offer breakthroughs in fields like cryptography, artificial intelligence, and materials science, leading to advancements that are currently beyond our imagination.

Applications and Current Status of Quantum Computing

Quantum computing might have a huge impact on the technology and society in the future. Often technologies like this are overestimated in the short run and underestimated in the long run. As once discussed in one of my podcasts with Professor Hanson of the technical university in delft, the netherlands, the usage of quantum is still unknown and we are really in the beginning of the technology where we are maturing the technology and looking for applications and usage of these quantum computers. Also don't forget the idea of quantum technology to actually build the new quantum internet. Lets dive into some of the potential applications.

Quantum Computing in Drug Discovery

One of the most promising applications of quantum computing is in the field of drug discovery. The interaction of molecules is fundamentally a quantum problem. Current classical simulation methods often require simplifications that could miss potential breakthroughs. Quantum computers could simulate molecular structures with high accuracy, opening the door for discovering new drugs or materials with unprecedented properties. Companies like IBM and startups in the quantum space are already partnering with pharmaceutical giants to push this application forward.

Breaking and Making Codes: Cryptography

Quantum computing poses both a risk and an opportunity for the field of cryptography. Algorithms like Shor's could theoretically break current encryption methods used to secure the internet. However, the same technology could lead to quantum-safe encryption methods. Research is underway to develop cryptographic algorithms that would be secure even in the age of quantum computing, often termed as "post-quantum cryptography."

Financial Modeling and Risk Assessment

Financial institutions deal with complex models to predict market trends and assess risks. These models often involve a multitude of variables and require a significant amount of computational power. Quantum algorithms could analyze these complex models much more efficiently than classical methods, providing more accurate risk assessments and potentially uncovering new financial opportunities. Companies like JPMorgan Chase are already exploring these capabilities in partnership with quantum computing firms.

Supply Chain and Logistics

Quantum computing could revolutionize the optimization problems associated with supply chain management and logistics. Whether it's determining the most efficient route for delivery trucks or optimizing the stocking of items in a warehouse, quantum algorithms could provide solutions that are not just incrementally better but qualitatively different. Industries from retail to manufacturing stand to gain from these advancements.

Artificial Intelligence and Machine Learning

Quantum computing could also accelerate the field of artificial intelligence. Complex machine learning models that require extensive computational power could be trained more efficiently on a quantum processor. Quantum-enhanced machine learning could lead to faster data analysis, more accurate models, and, consequently, more intelligent AI systems.

In 2019, Google claimed to have achieved 'quantum supremacy' by performing a specific task faster than the world's most advanced classical computer. While the task was highly specialized and not practically useful, it was a significant milestone, demonstrating that quantum computing is not just theoretical but achievable. Since then, there have been several other milestones, including advances in quantum error correction and the development of more stable qubits.

Ongoing Projects and Investments

Governments and private institutions alike are investing heavily in quantum computing. The United States, China, and the European Union have all announced multi-billion-dollar plans to accelerate quantum research. Tech giants like IBM, Google, and Microsoft are competing with a host of startups like Rigetti Computing, IonQ, and D-Wave in a race to build scalable, practical quantum computers.

While the potential of quantum computing is immense, it's essential to temper expectations. Scalable, fault-tolerant quantum computers are still years, if not decades, away. However, we are likely to see specialized quantum processors for specific tasks much sooner. These 'quantum co-processors' could work in tandem with classical systems, providing quantum acceleration for particular problems.

Ethical, Societal, and Regulatory Considerations

As quantum computing technologies advance, they bring forth ethical questions that society must grapple with. For example, the potential to crack existing cryptographic systems raises concerns about privacy and data security. In a world increasingly reliant on digital communication, the power to decrypt securely transmitted information could be misused in numerous ways, from government surveillance to corporate espionage. These ethical challenges necessitate a robust framework for the responsible use of quantum computing.

Quantum computing has the potential to widen the technological gap between developed and developing nations. As we have seen with previous technological revolutions, those who adopt new technologies early often reap disproportionate benefits. If quantum computing solutions become the domain of a privileged few, they could exacerbate existing inequalities on both a national and global scale. This calls for an inclusive approach to quantum technology development and deployment, ensuring that its benefits are accessible to a broad spectrum of society.

The regulatory environment for quantum computing is still in its nascent stages. Given the technology's ability to disrupt multiple sectors, from finance to national security, a comprehensive regulatory framework is crucial. Such a framework should cover not only the ethical use of the technology but also issues related to data privacy, antitrust considerations, and even international relations. The global nature of quantum computing—with researchers, companies, and governments across the world invested in its development—also raises questions about jurisdiction and governance on an international scale.

Quantum computing offers new avenues for both enhancing and compromising data privacy. On the one hand, quantum encryption methods could provide unprecedented levels of data security. On the other hand, the ability to break existing encryption algorithms poses significant privacy risks. Balancing these opposing forces will require new data protection legislation that addresses the unique capabilities of quantum computing.

National Security Concerns

The implications of quantum computing for national security are significant. Quantum technologies could revolutionize secure communications, data analysis, and even remote sensing, offering advantages in intelligence operations and national defense. However, the same technologies could also pose risks if misused or if they fall into the wrong hands. This necessitates a coordinated approach between governments, academia, and industry to ensure the responsible development and deployment of quantum technologies in the context of national security.

As research in quantum computing accelerates, ethical considerations must be integrated into the research and development process. This includes responsible data management, ethical treatment of intellectual property, and the consideration of the long-term societal impacts of the technology. Collaborative efforts, such as the Quantum Community Network and various academic consortiums, are making strides in this direction, but much work remains to be done.

As quantum computing becomes increasingly integrated into various industries, there will be a growing demand for a workforce skilled in quantum technologies. Preparing for this future requires investment in educational programs, ranging from K-12 to higher education and professional training. Public awareness and understanding of quantum computing are also crucial for informed public discourse on the ethical, societal, and regulatory challenges it presents.

Chapter 4: The Evolution and Status of Artificial Intelligence

The quest to develop intelligent machines dates back to the early days of computing. Initial efforts in AI were rooted in symbolic logic, aiming to create rule-based systems that could mimic human decision-making. The focus was on explicit programming to solve problems like chess playing or natural language understanding. However, these 'good old-fashioned AI' systems had limitations—they were brittle, not easily scalable, and unable to deal with the complexity of the real world.

The concept of artificial neural networks—systems inspired by the structure and function of the human brain—was introduced as early as the 1940s but gained traction in the 1980s and 1990s. The development of learning algorithms for these networks paved the way for machine learning, a subfield of AI that focuses on enabling machines to learn from data rather than being explicitly programmed. This shift marked a significant turning point in AI research, laying the groundwork for the deep learning revolution that would follow. Since AI is been used as a "container" word its better to open the box and look at the different technologies to understand the potential and limitations.

Deep Learning: A Leap Forward

Deep learning, a subset of machine learning involving neural networks with three or more layers, has led to breakthroughs in various AI applications, from image and speech recognition to natural language processing. The advent of big data and advancements in computational power have fueled this progress, making it possible to train increasingly complex models. Deep learning has largely shaped our current understanding of AI, powering technologies like self-driving cars, virtual assistants, and advanced recommendation systems.

Narrow AI vs. General AI

So far, most AI systems have been 'narrow AI,' specialized in performing specific tasks. In contrast, Artificial General Intelligence (AGI) would have the ability to understand, learn, and adapt across a wide range of tasks, much like a human. While AGI remains a theoretical concept, the focus of AI research and development has primarily been on narrow AI, aiming to solve real-world problems in various domains.

Human-Centered AI

As AI systems become more capable, there's a growing emphasis on human-centered AI, which focuses on the symbiotic relationship between humans and machines. This approach aims to design AI systems that not only augment human capabilities but also align with human values and ethics. Human-centered AI is becoming increasingly relevant as AI starts to impact critical areas like healthcare, governance, and employment.

AI in Popular Imagination

From Hollywood blockbusters to dystopian literature, AI has been a subject of fascination and fear in popular culture. While these portrayals often exaggerate the capabilities and risks associated with AI, they reflect underlying societal attitudes and concerns. These perceptions have, to some extent, influenced the discourse around AI ethics, regulation, and societal impact.

The Business Perspective

From our early interactions with AI at various industry conferences and publications, to our present-day involvement in AI projects, the business community has shown increasing interest in leveraging AI for competitive advantage. Whether it's automating customer service, enhancing data analytics, or driving innovation in product development, AI is now considered a cornerstone of digital transformation strategies across industries.

Applications and Impact: From Theory to Practice

There are many potential cases on a theoretical as well as a practical level throughout all different industries. Chapter 6 will elaborate in more detail on the potential and innovation possibilities. Overall we see theory already been translated into practical cases with impressive results. As explained in our introduction, we are just at the start of the real potential and adoption.

Healthcare: Diagnostics and Beyond

Artificial Intelligence has made significant strides in healthcare, revolutionizing how we diagnose, treat, and manage diseases. Machine learning algorithms can analyze medical images with high accuracy, often outperforming human experts. AI-driven predictive analytics are also being employed to forecast out-breaks and the progression of diseases, enabling more proactive healthcare management.

Finance: Risk Assessment to Robo-Advisors

In the financial sector, AI has been a game-changer in risk assessment, fraud detection, and even investment manage-ment. Algorithms can analyze market data in real-time to make investment recommendations, and robo-advisors are becoming increasingly popular among retail investors. Ad-ditionally, machine learning models are deployed to detect fraudulent transactions, offering an extra layer of security in digital banking.

Retail and E-commerce: Personalization at Scale

AI algorithms analyze customer behavior and preferences to offer a highly personalized shopping experience. Whether it's recommending products or optimizing pricing strategies, AI has become an integral part of modern retail and e-commerce. Chat-bots, often powered by AI, provide customer service, assisting users and guiding them through the purchasing process.

Automotive: The Drive Towards Autonomy

Self-driving cars have been a staple of science fiction for years, but thanks to AI, they are becoming a reality. While fully autonomous vehicles are still in the development phase, many modern cars come equipped with AI-powered features like lane-keeping assist, adaptive cruise control, and automated parking.

Media and Entertainment: Content Generation and Curation

AI is also making its mark in the media and entertainment sectors. Algorithms curate personalized playlists, recommend movies or articles, and even help in content creation. For example, AI algorithms can analyze user engagement metrics to recommend editorial topics or identify trending stories.

Social Impact: AI for Good

Beyond commercial applications, AI is being used to address some of the world's most pressing challenges. Projects leveraging AI for social good range from using machine learning to predict natural disasters to deploying AI algorithms for wildlife conservation. These initiatives reflect the technology's potential to drive positive societal change.

The Future of Work: Automation and Augmentation

One of the most hotly debated impacts of AI is its effect on employment. While automation threatens to displace workers in some sectors, AI also offers opportunities for job augmentation. For instance, AI tools can handle repetitive tasks, freeing up human workers to focus on more creative and complex activities. The key lies in finding a balance and ensuring that the workforce is reskilled to adapt to an AI-augmented environment.

Ethical and Regulatory Impact

As AI systems become more pervasive, they also raise ethical and regulatory questions, such as those related to data privacy, algorithmic bias, and decision transparency. Governing bodies and organizations are in the early stages of establishing frameworks and guidelines to ensure the ethical deployment of AI.

The rise of AI is not merely a technological revolution but a societal one. Its applications span across industries, affecting how we live, work, and interact. This transformative potential makes AI one of the cornerstone technologies of the current era, deserving of the focused attention it is receiving from both the business and academic communities.

Challenges and Limitations: The Road Ahead

One of the most significant challenges in AI is its heavy reliance on data. Machine learning models, particularly deep learning, require massive amounts of data for training. The availability and quality of this data can significantly impact the performance of AI systems. In some cases, the data might be imbalanced or biased, leading to skewed results.

AI systems, especially complex neural networks, are often criticized for being "black boxes," meaning their decision-making processes are not easily interpretable by humans. This lack of explainability is a significant concern, especially in critical applications like healthcare or criminal justice, where understanding the reasoning behind decisions is crucial.

Most current AI systems are specialized in performing specific tasks and struggle to generalize their learning to new, but related, tasks. Developing AI systems capable of transfer learning—applying knowledge from one domain to another—is an ongoing area of research.

Societal and Ethical Challenges

AI systems can inherit biases present in their training data or their designers. These biases can perpetuate existing social inequalities when deployed in real-world scenarios, such as hiring, lending, or law enforcement.

While AI has the potential to augment human capabilities, there's also a valid concern about job displacement due to automation. Industries with repetitive tasks are particularly vulnerable, raising questions about workforce retraining and economic inequality.

AI systems are not immune to security risks. From adversarial attacks that fool machine learning models to the ethical hacking of AI-powered systems, the security implications are vast and require concerted efforts to address.

AI Hallucination

In recent years, we've seen a rise in the phenomenon of AI hallucination, where artificial intelligence systems fabricate stories or details that seem incredibly real and plausible, yet are entirely false. Picture a virtual assistant that spontaneously creates a news article filled with compelling anecdotes, supporting quotes, and intricate details, all based on patterns it learned during its training from the vast sea of information on the internet. While these narratives may be rich and engaging, they can stray far from the truth, essentially "hallucinating" facts and events that do not exist. For business executives, this presents a twofold challenge: on one hand, it becomes increasingly difficult to differentiate between authentic and artificial content, risking decision-making based on false information. On the other hand, it offers an avenue for creative and innovative applications in content creation, advertising, and more. Navigating this landscape necessitates a discerning approach to information consumption and a deep understanding of the strengths and weaknesses of AI technologies. It emphasizes the unyielding value of critical thinking and verification in the AI-assisted business landscape.

Regulatory Challenges

As AI systems often require access to sensitive data, robust data governance mechanisms are essential. Regulations like GDPR in the European Union are a step in the right direction but navigating the global regulatory landscape remains a challenge.

The lack of standardized best practices for AI development and deployment is a growing concern. Questions about who is accountable when an AI system makes a wrong decision, intentionally or not, are still up for debate.

In line with the themes we've explored it's evident that while AI offers transformative potential, it also presents complex challenges that require multi-faceted solutions. Addressing these challenges isn't just a technological endeavor but also a societal, ethical, and regulatory imperative.

Chapter 5: The Rise of Generative AI

enerative AI refers to a class of algorithms designed to create new data that is similar to some existing data. While traditional AI models are often used for tasks like classification or prediction, generative models aim to produce content. This can range from generating text and images to creating music and even simulating various forms of human-like interaction. In the last years i have often presented and published on the concept of AI components where individual elements of AI have grown mature and very usable. AI components such as Computer Vision, Language recognition, Video recognition, Language translations. The missing link always was the generative or "reason" part that can actually understand the context of what other components recognize and detect and can translate this into actions. "Reason" also comes close to the concept of being human since it implies intelligence. If computers can reason, what differentiates us from a computer? For now lets come back to the technology of generative AI and explore what its all about.

From GANs to Transformers: The Technology Behind Generative AI

The technology powering generative models is continually evolving. Generative Adversarial Networks (GANs) have been instrumental in creating realistic images and videos. On the text generation front, Transformer architectures, like the one that powers this very document, have set new benchmarks in generating human-like text. The progress in this subfield of AI has been rapid, powered by advancements in machine learning techniques and computational power.

Applications: Beyond Deepfakes and Chatbots

While Generative AI has gained notoriety for its role in creating deepfakes, its applications are far more varied and constructive. For instance, generative algorithms are being used in drug discovery, where they can simulate molecular structures for new medications. They are also used in creative fields like art and music, often in collaboration with human artists. In customer service, advanced chatbots powered by Generative AI can handle complex queries, providing a more efficient and pleasant experience for users.

Generative AI in Business

Businesses are starting to realize the potential of Generative AI in various operational aspects. Whether it's automating content creation for marketing campaigns or generating code for software development, the technology offers ways to enhance productivity and creativity. Generative AI represents a significant shift in how businesses can leverage AI for innovation and efficiency.

Ethical Considerations

Like other AI technologies, Generative AI brings its own set of ethical questions. The ability to generate realistic content poses challenges related to misinformation, data privacy, and intellectual property. As generative models become more advanced, the need for ethical guidelines and regulations becomes increasingly urgent.

Challenges and Limitations

While Generative AI holds enormous promise, it also faces challenges related to data dependency, computational costs, and the risk of generating harmful or misleading content. These challenges are not insurmountable but do require focused research and ethical considerations.

Use-Cases and Transformative Potential

With generative AI we feel even more then ever before the impact it has and can have on businesses and jobs. I have published about this for the last years always explaining that on the long run the impact might even be bigger then we think. Smart machines in physical form might replace physical oriented jobs with physical work. Smart machines such as generative AI has their primary impact on office and information workers. Lets look at some of the potential domains where generative AI will have a big impact.

Media and Journalism: Automated Content Generation
Generative AI is making waves in the media industry by automating content generation. From summarizing articles to producing news reports based on data, these algorithms can significantly speed up the content creation process. However, the rise of automated journalism also poses ethical questions around bias and accountability.

Healthcare: Generating Medical Data

In healthcare, Generative AI models are being used to create synthetic medical data for research. This synthetic data can help researchers develop new treatments and diagnostic methods without compromising patient privacy. It also opens up the potential for personalized medicine, where treatments are tailored to individual genetic profiles.

Marketing: Personalized Content at Scale

Generative AI is a powerful tool for marketers, enabling the automated creation of personalized content. Whether it's email campaigns, social media posts, or even personalized video messages, Generative AI can create content that resonates with individual consumers, enhancing engagement and customer loyalty.

Arts and Culture: AI as a Creative Partner

Artists and musicians are exploring the use of Generative AI as a creative tool. Algorithms can generate melodies, paint landscapes, and even write poetry. While this raises questions about authorship and creativity, it also offers exciting possibilities for human–AI collaboration in artistic endeavors.

Scientific Research: Simulating Complex Systems

Generative AI is finding applications in scientific research, particularly in fields that require the simulation of complex systems. For example, it's being used in climate modeling, where it can generate detailed simulations to predict future climate changes. Similarly, in astrophysics, Generative AI can simulate celestial phenomena, aiding in our understanding of the universe.

E-commerce: Virtual Try-Ons and Product Customization

In the e-commerce sector, Generative AI is being used to offer virtual try-ons and personalized product recommendations. Customers can see how clothes will look on them or how furniture will fit in their homes before making a purchase, significantly enhancing the online shopping experience.

Legal Sector: Document Drafting and Review

Generative AI is also making inroads into the legal sector. Algorithms can draft contracts, review legal documents, and even predict the outcomes of legal cases based on historical data.

This not only speeds up the legal process but also minimizes human error.

Real-World Cases from Our Portfolio

In line with the trends we've been discussing in our previous publications, we've witnessed firsthand the transformative potential of Generative AI. Whether it's automating business processes or driving innovation in product design, the technology has proven to be a valuable asset in our portfolio of AI solutions.

Ethical, Societal, and Regulatory Challenges

One of the most immediate concerns with Generative AI is its potential to create convincing fake content, such as deepfake videos or fabricated news articles. The ability to generate such content could have serious implications for misinformation, fraud, and even national security. It's vital to develop detection methods and ethical guidelines to combat the malicious use of generative technologies.

Generative AI's ability to produce original content poses questions around intellectual property and authorship. Who owns the rights to a song generated by an AI? Is an artwork created by a machine eligible for copyright? These are complex questions that require rethinking existing intellectual property laws and conventions.

Generative AI models are often trained on large datasets that may include sensitive or personal information. Even if the generated content is synthetic, the question remains: How can we ensure the privacy and ethical use of the data used to train these models? Data governance becomes a critical concern here.

Like other AI models, generative models are susceptible to inheriting the biases present in their training data. Ensuring that these technologies are inclusive and free from prejudice is a significant ethical challenge. This is particularly important in applications like content generation and personalization, where biased algorithms could perpetuate existing social inequalities.

The rapid advancements in Generative AI outpace existing regulatory frameworks. Governing bodies are grappling with how to regulate the ethical and responsible use of this technology. Given its transformative and potentially disruptive nature, a multi-stakeholder approach involving technologists, policymakers, and ethicists is crucial for crafting effective regulations.

The societal impact of Generative AI extends beyond regulatory and ethical concerns. How ready is society to accept machine-generated content, especially in domains traditionally considered human-centric, like arts and journalism? Public perception and acceptance will play a significant role in how these technologies are integrated into daily life.

From Our Lens: A Balanced Approach

As we've emphasized in our previous presentations, tackling the challenges posed by Generative AI requires a balanced approach. Technical solutions must be complemented by ethical guidelines, societal dialogue, and regulatory oversight. It's not merely about what the technology can do but also about what it should do, underlining the need for responsible innovation.

Chapter 6: Industries and Sectors: Navigating the Impact of the Smart Machine Age

After entering the Smart Machine age years ago we see in everyday life the increasing impact of the technologies discussed before. What could potentially be the impact that these technologies will have on business and society.

Healthcare: From Diagnosis to Treatment

Healthcare is undergoing a transformative shift, aided by the infusion of cutting-edge technologies like Artificial Intelligence (AI) and quantum computing. These advancements are not mere incremental changes; they promise to redefine everything from diagnosis to treatment and beyond. As we've discussed in our previous publications and presentations, these technologies are poised to drastically impact healthcare, making this an opportune moment to delve into the particulars.

One of the most prominent applications of AI in healthcare is in the realm of diagnostics. Traditional diagnostic methods often rely on human expertise and can be time-consuming. AI, particularly machine learning algorithms, can analyze complex medical images, such as MRIs and X-rays, often with greater accuracy and in a fraction of the time it would take a human expert. These algorithms are continually learning, improving their diagnostic accuracy as more data becomes available.

Quantum computing promises to revolutionize drug discovery by simulating molecular interactions at an unprecedented scale and speed. This capability could dramatically accelerate the time it takes to bring a new drug to market, potentially saving countless lives. Quantum algorithms can sift through enormous datasets to identify likely drug candidates, perform complex simulations to predict their effects, and even optimize manufacturing processes to produce them more efficiently.

AI's capacity to analyze vast datasets allows for personalized treatment plans. By evaluating a patient's medical history, genetic makeup, and even lifestyle factors, AI algorithms can recommend treatments that are most likely to be effective for the individual patient. This move toward personalized medicine could improve treatment outcomes and reduce healthcare costs by eliminating less effective treatments.

As healthcare systems generate increasing amounts of data, effective data management becomes critical. AI can automate many aspects of healthcare data management, including the organization and analysis of patient records. Quantum computing could take this a step further by enabling new forms of encryption, ensuring that sensitive medical data remains secure while still being accessible for analysis and sharing across platforms.

As with any technology, AI and quantum computing introduce ethical considerations. Patient data, being sensitive by nature, needs to be handled with utmost care to respect privacy norms. Moreover, machine learning algorithms can inherit biases present in their training data. If not properly addressed, these biases could lead to healthcare disparities, undermining the potential benefits of these technologies.

Regulatory Landscape: Balancing Innovation and Safety

The rapid advancements in AI and quantum computing outpace existing regulatory frameworks, making it challenging to ensure that these technologies are both innovative and safe. Regulatory bodies are beginning to acknowledge the need for new laws and standards that address the unique challenges and opportunities presented by these technologies. The focus is on ensuring data privacy, validating the reliability of AI algorithms, and setting guidelines for the ethical use of technology in healthcare settings.

Preparing the Healthcare Workforce

The implementation of AI and quantum computing in healthcare will require a workforce that is skilled in both medical practice and technology. Interdisciplinary education programs that integrate medical sciences with computational skills are becoming increasingly essential. Healthcare professionals need to be trained to collaborate with technologists to ensure that the technology is implemented in a manner that is both effective and ethical.

The Future Outlook: Integrated and Intelligent Healthcare Ecosystems

Looking ahead, we can envision a healthcare ecosystem that is deeply integrated with AI and quantum computing technologies. Diagnostics will become more accurate and faster, treatment plans more personalized, and healthcare data more secure and interoperable. All of these advancements have the potential to improve healthcare outcomes and reduce costs, making quality healthcare more accessible to people around the world.

As AI and quantum computing technologies mature, their impact on healthcare is becoming increasingly profound. While the benefits are numerous, from improved diagnostics to personalized treatments, challenges remain. These include ethical considerations, the need for updated regulatory frameworks, and the necessity of preparing the healthcare workforce for a technologically advanced future. As we've often emphasized, navigating these challenges successfully will require a balanced, multi-disciplinary approach.

Financial Services: Risk, Rewards, and Regulation

The financial services sector has always been at the forefront of adopting new technologies, and AI and quantum computing are no exceptions. The industry is characterized by complex transactions, massive data sets, and a high demand for security and accuracy—all of which make it ripe for technological disruption. As we've pointed out before, the financial sector is among the most likely to be profoundly impacted by these emerging technologies.

AI in Fraud Detection: The New Security Guard

Fraud detection is one of the most immediate applications of AI in the financial sector. Traditional methods rely heavily on rule-based systems and manual reviews, which can be time-consuming and error-prone. AI algorithms, particularly those using machine learning, can analyze enormous sets of transactional data in real-time to identify suspicious activities. The advantage lies in the system's ability to learn from new instances of fraud, making it increasingly effective over time.

Quantum Computing in Risk Assessment: Changing the Game

Risk assessment in finance involves complex models and calculations that can be computationally intensive. Quantum computing has the potential to perform these calculations exponentially faster than classical computers. This speed can revolutionize areas such as credit scoring, portfolio optimization, and even insurance underwriting, making financial services more efficient and potentially more equitable.

Investment and Trading: The Rise of Robo-Advisors

AI-driven robo-advisors are increasingly popular in the financial sector, especially among retail investors. These algorithms analyze market data and investor preferences to offer personalized investment strategies. Quantum computing could take this a step further by solving complex market models in real-time, offering even more accurate and timely investment advice.

Customer Service: Chatbots and Beyond

Customer service in financial institutions is becoming increasingly automated, thanks to AI. Chatbots and virtual assistants can handle a variety of tasks from answering frequently asked questions to guiding users through complex financial transactions. As natural language processing technologies continue to improve, these automated systems are becoming more sophisticated and capable of handling complex customer interactions.

Regulatory Compliance: AI to the Rescue

Compliance with financial regulations is a significant challenge for institutions, requiring substantial resources for data collection, reporting, and audits. AI can automate many of these processes, analyzing transactional data to ensure compliance with various regulations like AML (Anti-Money Laundering) and KYC (Know Your Customer). Quantum computing could further enhance these capabilities by enabling encrypted, secure computations that comply with data privacy regulations.

Ethical and Regulatory Challenges: A Balancing Act

The use of AI and quantum computing in financial services raises several ethical and regulatory challenges. Data security and privacy are paramount, especially given the sensitive nature of financial data. Moreover, the use of algorithms for tasks like credit scoring and investment advising raises questions about accountability and bias. Regulatory bodies are beginning to grapple with these issues, working to establish frameworks that balance innovation with consumer protection.

The Workforce Transformation: Reskilling and Upskilling

As AI and quantum computing become more integrated into financial services, the nature of work will inevitably change. While there's concern over job displacement due to automation, there's also a growing need for a workforce skilled in both financial services and emerging technologies. Upskilling programs focusing on data science, machine learning, and quantum computing fundamentals are becoming crucial for career longevity in the sector.

The Future Outlook: A Financial Ecosystem Transformed

Looking ahead, the financial services sector is poised for a transformation unlike any seen before. The integration of AI and quantum computing will make services faster, more efficient, and potentially more equitable. However, these advancements will also bring challenges in ethics, regulation, and workforce preparedness that must be thoughtfully addressed.

The financial services sector stands on the brink of a technological revolution driven by AI and quantum computing. These technologies offer unprecedented efficiencies and open new avenues for service delivery and product innovation. However, they also pose challenges that the industry must navigate carefully. Regulatory frameworks need to evolve, ethical considerations must be at the forefront, and a future-ready workforce needs to be developed.

Manufacturing and Supply Chain: Efficiency and Optimization

The manufacturing and supply chain sectors are undergoing a digital transformation, driven by advancements in AI and quantum computing. The industry's core—built on physical processes and logistical efficiency—is ripe for digital disruption. These technologies have the potential to drive unprecedented levels of efficiency, accuracy, and innovation in the sector.

AI-Powered Predictive Maintenance: A Revolution in Asset Management

One of the most immediate applications of AI in manufacturing is predictive maintenance. Traditional maintenance schedules are often based on time intervals or usage metrics, which can result in unnecessary downtime or unexpected failures. AI algorithms can analyze real-time data from machinery sensors to predict when maintenance is actually needed. This not only extends the life of the equipment but also reduces downtime and associated costs.

Quantum Computing in Supply Chain Optimization: The Next Frontier

Supply chain optimization is a complex problem involving multiple variables such as inventory levels, transportation logistics, and demand forecasts. Traditional optimization methods can take considerable time and computational power. Quantum computing can solve these problems in a fraction of the time, leading to more efficient supply chain operations and potentially saving billions of dollars annually.

Process Automation and AI: The New Production Line

AI technologies are increasingly being used to automate various aspects of the manufacturing process, from sorting and packaging to quality control. Computer vision algorithms can identify defects in products faster and more accurately than human inspectors. Robotics powered by AI can handle tasks that are dangerous or repetitive, improving both safety and efficiency on the factory floor.

Real-Time Inventory Management: AI Takes Charge

Managing inventory in real-time is a challenging task that AI is well-equipped to handle. Algorithms can analyze sales data, monitor stock levels, and even predict future demand to optimize inventory levels. This not only reduces carrying costs but also improves service levels by ensuring that products are available when customers need them.

Workforce Training and Upskilling: Preparing for the Future

The integration of AI and quantum computing technologies into manufacturing processes will inevitably require a new set of skills from the workforce. Training programs focusing on understanding these technologies and their applications in manufacturing are essential. While there may be concerns about job displacement due to automation, the focus is shifting toward upskilling workers to operate and manage these advanced systems.

Ethical and Environmental Considerations: Beyond Profitability

As manufacturing processes become more efficient and automated, ethical and environmental considerations come into focus. AI algorithms should be designed to optimize not just for profitability but also for environmental sustainability. Quantum computing could be used to model and optimize energy-efficient processes, contributing to more sustainable manufacturing practices.

Regulatory Compliance and Data Security: Navigating Complexity

The use of advanced technologies like AI and quantum computing introduces new layers of complexity in terms of regulatory compliance and data security. Manufacturing plants often have strict regulations related to safety, data handling, and environmental impact. Ensuring that these new technologies comply with existing laws while also preparing for future regulatory landscapes is a significant challenge.

The Future Outlook: A Paradigm Shift in Manufacturing and Supply Chain

Looking ahead, the manufacturing and supply chain sectors are set for a paradigm shift. AI and quantum computing offer the promise of highly optimized, efficient, and flexible operations. However, they also bring challenges related to workforce adaptation, regulatory compliance, and ethical considerations.

The manufacturing and supply chain sectors are on the cusp of a technological revolution. The integration of AI and quantum computing technologies promises to transform these industries, driving efficiencies and opening up new avenues for innovation. However, this transformation is not without its challenges. Navigating the road ahead will require a balanced approach that considers not just technological capabilities but also ethical, regulatory, and workforce-related challenges.

Retail and E-commerce: Personalization and Prediction

The retail and e-commerce sectors are undergoing a profound transformation, fueled by advancements in AI and quantum computing. This transformation is both a challenge and an opportunity for retailers to reimagine their business models.

AI-Driven Personalization: The New Normal

One of the most transformative applications of AI in retail is personalization. Gone are the days when one-size-fits-all marketing strategies were effective. Today's consumers expect personalized experiences, and AI algorithms are making this possible by analyzing data on shopping behavior, preferences, and even social media activity. These algorithms can recommend products, offer personalized discounts, and even predict future purchases, thereby increasing both customer satisfaction and sales.

Quantum Computing in Consumer Behavior Analysis

Quantum computing has the potential to take consumer behavior analysis to the next level. By rapidly analyzing complex sets of data, quantum algorithms can identify subtle patterns and correlations that classical computing methods might miss. This could lead to even more effective personalization strategies, where promotions and products are tailored to individual consumer profiles with unprecedented accuracy.

Real-Time Inventory Management: The Quantum Advantage

Managing inventory in real-time is a significant challenge for retailers. AI algorithms can automate much of this work by analyzing sales data and adjusting stock levels accordingly. Quantum computing can take this a step further by solving complex optimization problems related to supply chain logistics and warehouse management, potentially saving millions in operational costs.

Customer Service: AI Chatbots and Beyond

AI is revolutionizing customer service in retail, with chatbots now capable of handling a range of tasks from answering FAQs to processing returns. As natural language processing technologies improve, these chatbots are becoming increasingly sophisticated, offering a more human-like interaction experience. Quantum computing could further enhance these capabilities by enabling real-time analysis of customer sentiment and preferences.

Ethical Considerations: Data Privacy and Algorithmic Bias

As with any technology, the use of AI and quantum computing in retail raises ethical questions. Data privacy is a significant concern, especially given the amount of personal information that algorithms analyze. Additionally, there's the risk of algorithmic bias, where the AI system might favor or discriminate against certain groups based on the data it has been trained on.

Regulatory Challenges: Navigating a Complex Landscape

The rapid advancements in technology often outpace existing regulatory frameworks. Retailers must navigate a complicated set of rules related to data protection, consumer rights, and even environmental sustainability. As AI and quantum computing become more integrated into retail operations, new regulations are likely to emerge, requiring retailers to stay agile and informed.

Preparing the Retail Workforce: Upskilling for the Future

The integration of AI and quantum computing into retail will undoubtedly require a new skill set from the workforce. Employees will need to be trained in data analytics, machine learning, and possibly even quantum mechanics to effectively interact with these new systems. While this represents a challenge, it's also an opportunity for workforce development and upskilling.

Looking ahead, we can envision a retail ecosystem that seamlessly integrates online and offline experiences, all powered by AI and quantum computing technologies. Inventory will be optimized, consumer interactions will be personalized, and new levels of efficiency will be achieved. However, this future also brings with it challenges related to ethics, regulation, and workforce adaptation that must be thoughtfully navigated.

Energy and Utilities: Sustainability and Smart Grids

The energy and utilities sectors are at a crossroads, facing challenges related to sustainability, efficiency, and the rising demand for clean energy. AI and quantum computing offer groundbreaking solutions to these challenges.

AI in Smart Grids: A New Dawn for Energy Management

Smart grids represent one of the most promising applications of AI in the energy sector. These grids use AI algorithms to analyze real-time data from various sensors, enabling dynamic pricing and optimizing energy distribution. The result is not only more efficient energy use but also a more resilient and adaptive energy infrastructure.

Quantum Computing in Renewable Energy: Material Science and Beyond

The development of new materials for efficient energy storage and transmission is a significant challenge in renewable energy research. Quantum computing can simulate molecular structures at an unprecedented scale, potentially accelerating the discovery of new materials for batteries, solar cells, and other renewable energy technologies.

Energy Efficiency: AI's Role in Demand Forecasting

AI algorithms can analyze vast sets of historical and real-time data to forecast energy demand accurately. This is crucial for optimizing energy production and reducing waste. Accurate demand forecasting can also help in better management of renewable energy sources, aligning production with actual needs.

Sustainable Energy Production: Quantum Algorithms for Optimization

Optimizing the mix of energy sources for sustainable energy production is a complex problem. Quantum computing has the potential to solve these complex optimization problems much faster than classical computers, enabling more effective use of renewable sources like wind, solar, and hydroelectric power.

Ethical and Environmental Considerations: The Double-Edged Sword

While AI and quantum computing offer potential solutions to environmental challenges, their operations also consume significant amounts of energy. Ethical considerations around the energy consumption of these technologies themselves must be part of the discussion on their application in the energy sector.

Regulatory Challenges: Old Laws, New Technologies

The use of AI and quantum computing in energy and utilities presents a complex regulatory landscape. These technologies have the potential to disrupt established industry practices and regulatory frameworks. As they become more integrated into the sector, new regulations that address their unique challenges and opportunities are likely to emerge.

Workforce Adaptation: Training for a Technological Future

The integration of AI and quantum computing technologies into the energy sector will necessitate a new set of skills from the workforce. Training programs focusing on data analytics, machine learning, and even quantum mechanics are becoming essential for workers in this sector.

Future Outlook: A Holistic, Sustainable Energy Ecosystem

The future of the energy and utilities sector is likely to be characterized by a holistic approach that incorporates AI and quantum computing at multiple levels. From smart grids that optimize energy distribution to quantum algorithms that facilitate the discovery of new sustainable materials, the future is bright but comes with its own set of challenges.

The energy and utilities sectors stand at the threshold of a technological revolution. AI and quantum computing offer transformative solutions but also present challenges that require thoughtful navigation. The road ahead is fraught with both opportunities and obstacles that will require a balanced approach.

Education: Personalized Learning and Advanced Research

The education sector is experiencing profound changes, driven by technological advancements like AI and quantum computing. As we've highlighted in our previous publications, these tech‑nologies hold the potential to redefine educational experiences and outcomes.

AI in Personalized Learning: A Paradigm Shift

One of the most exciting applications of AI in education is personalized learning. Traditional educational models often take a one-size-fits-all approach, which fails to account for individual learning styles, paces, and preferences. AI algorithms can analyze student performance and adapt learning materials and exercises to suit individual needs, thereby making education more personalized and effective.

Quantum Computing in Advanced Research: A New Frontier

Quantum computing is set to revolutionize research method‑ologies in various disciplines, including physics, chemistry, and even social sciences. The ability to perform complex computations at unprecedented speeds can accelerate research projects, offering quicker insights and breakthroughs.

Data Analytics for Educational Outcomes

AI has a significant role in analyzing educational data to improve outcomes. Algorithms can sift through test scores, attendance records, and even social and emotional cues to identify trends, challenges, and opportunities for improvement. This data-driven approach enables educators and policymakers to make informed decisions that can shape the future of education.

Virtual and Augmented Reality: Enhanced Learning Experiences

AI-powered virtual and augmented reality systems can provide immersive learning experiences. These technologies can simulate real-world scenarios for practical learning, from scientific experiments to historical events, thereby enriching the educational experience.

Ethical Considerations: Data Privacy and Algorithmic Bias

The use of AI and quantum computing in education raises several ethical questions. The most pressing among these are data privacy and algorithmic bias. Sensitive student data must be handled carefully to ensure privacy. Moreover, algorithms must be designed to be as unbiased as possible to ensure that all students have equal learning opportunities.

Regulatory Challenges: Education in the Age of AI

The rapid incorporation of AI and quantum computing into educational systems poses regulatory challenges. Curriculum guidelines, teacher training, and data usage policies must be updated to incorporate these new technologies responsibly.

Workforce Training and Skill Development: Preparing Educators

The successful integration of AI and quantum computing into education requires a skilled workforce. Teachers and educators will need training in data analytics, machine learning, and the ethical implications of these technologies. This need for up-skilling is both a challenge and an opportunity for professional development.

The future classroom is likely to be a blend of physical and virtual learning environments, powered by AI algorithms and possibly even quantum computers. These technologies promise to make education more personalized, efficient, and globally accessible. However, they also bring challenges in ethics, regulation, and workforce adaptation that must be carefully navigated.

The education sector is on the cusp of a technological revolution. The integration of AI and quantum computing into educational systems offers transformative potential but also presents challenges requiring careful consideration. The path forward is complex but laden with opportunities for those prepared to navigate it responsibly.

Public Sector and Government: Reimagining Governance

The integration of AI and quantum computing technologies promises to reshape the very fabric of governance. The public sector stands to gain immensely from these advancements, although not without challenges.

Taxation: AI-driven Compliance and Fraud Detection

One of the primary roles of the government is the collection of taxes. AI algorithms can significantly improve tax compliance and fraud detection by analyzing complex financial data in real-time. For example, AI can sift through thousands of tax returns to flag inconsistencies, thereby aiding in quicker audits and reducing tax evasion. Quantum computing can further enhance these capabilities by solving complex optimization problems related to tax code application, potentially saving billions in lost revenue.

Infrastructure: Smart Cities and Quantum-Enhanced Planning

Infrastructure planning and maintenance are core government responsibilities. AI can manage and analyze data from various sensors placed throughout a city's infrastructure, ensuring optimal traffic flow, energy usage, and public safety. Quantum computing can handle the intricate calculations required for planning new infrastructure projects, evaluating millions of variables in a fraction of the time it would take traditional methods.

Social Security: Personalized Benefits and Fraud Prevention

Social security systems often suffer from inefficiencies and fraud. AI can personalize benefit schemes based on individual circumstances, ensuring equitable distribution. Additionally, machine learning algorithms can detect fraudulent claims with high accuracy. Quantum computing, with its ability to process complex simulations quickly, can model the long-term sustainability of social security programs, helping policymakers make informed decisions.

Public Safety: AI Surveillance and Quantum-Encoded Communications

In the realm of public safety, AI can analyze surveillance footage in real-time to identify potential threats or criminal activity. Quantum computing introduces the potential for quantum-encrypted communications that are practically impossible to intercept, thereby significantly enhancing national security measures.

Healthcare: Data-Driven Policies and Quantum Medical Research

Governments are increasingly relying on AI to analyze public health data for policymaking. For example, during the COVID-19 pandemic, AI models were used to predict the spread of the virus and the effectiveness of various interventions. Quantum computing could revolutionize medical research, enabling the rapid development of new drugs and treatment methods.

Ethical and Regulatory Landscapes: Navigating Complexity

The deployment of AI and quantum computing technologies in governance raises complex ethical and regulatory issues. Data privacy concerns, the potential for algorithmic bias, and questions surrounding quantum data security are among the challenges that must be navigated carefully.

Upskilling the Workforce: Preparing for a Technological Future

The integration of these cutting-edge technologies will require a public sector workforce trained in data analytics, machine learning, and quantum mechanics. This not only presents a challenge but also an opportunity for professional development and skills enhancement.

The transformation of the public sector through AI and quantum computing is not merely a theoretical concept; it's a burgeoning reality. This transformative journey is fraught with both opportunities and challenges. But the potential benefits—enhanced efficiency, greater equity, and more effective governance—are too significant to be ignored.

Chapter 7: Enabling Innovation and Transformation

As underscored in this book, the era of AI and quantum computing is upon us. Organizations that fail to adapt will find themselves at a competitive disadvantage. But how should companies begin this transformative journey?

Strategy Formulation: A Guiding Framework

A well-defined strategy serves as the north star for any technological transformation. It should align with the organization's overall business goals and take into account the specific challenges and opportunities presented by AI and quantum computing. Organizations should conduct a thorough SWOT analysis (Strengths, Weaknesses, Opportunities, Threats) focusing on these technologies.

Case Study: IBM's Quantum Strategy

For instance, IBM has been a leader in both AI and quantum computing, investing heavily in research and development. Their strategy focuses on creating an ecosystem around quantum computing, including partnerships with academic institutions and governments. This approach has positioned them as one of the forerunners in the field.

Building the Right Team: Skills and Expertise

The successful implementation of AI and quantum computing requires a multidisciplinary team with expertise in areas such as data analytics, machine learning, and quantum mechanics. This team should be diverse, including not just technologists but also experts in ethics, regulation, and business strategy.

Example: Google's Quantum AI Lab

Google's Quantum AI Lab serves as an excellent example. The lab employs researchers from various disciplines, including physics, computer science, and engineering, to work on both the hardware and software aspects of quantum computing.

Initial Investments: Hardware, Software, and Training

Adopting AI and quantum computing is a significant financial commitment. Organizations need to invest in hardware such as GPUs for machine learning or quantum processors, software licenses, and most importantly, training programs for their workforce.

Example: JPMorgan Chase's Investment in AI

JPMorgan Chase, a leading global financial services firm, has invested millions in AI to improve customer service, risk assessment, and fraud detection. They have also partnered with AI startups to stay ahead in the innovation curve.

Risk Assessment: Ethical and Regulatory Considerations

Before diving into implementation, organizations must assess the risks associated with adopting these technologies. Data privacy laws, such as GDPR in Europe, impose stringent requirements on data handling. Ethical considerations, such as algorithmic bias, must also be addressed proactively.

Case Study: Microsoft's Ethical AI Guidelines

Microsoft has published ethical guidelines for AI development and usage, emphasizing fairness, accountability, transparency, and ethics (FATE). These guidelines serve as a roadmap for other organizations to navigate the complex ethical landscape surrounding AI.

Pilot Projects: Small Steps, Big Learnings

Before a full-scale implementation, organizations should consider running pilot projects to test the waters. These projects provide invaluable insights into the practical challenges and benefits of implementing AI and quantum computing technologies.

Example: Walmart's AI-Powered Inventory Management

Walmart has successfully implemented AI-powered inventory management systems in select locations, leading to reduced stockouts and improved customer satisfaction. The success of these pilot projects has encouraged Walmart to scale the technology across its operations.

The journey towards adopting AI and quantum computing is complex but rewarding. A well-defined strategy, the right team, and thoughtful investments lay the foundation for success. Companies should also consider the ethical and regulatory implications of these technologies and start with pilot projects to gain practical insights.

Key Takeaways

- Formulate a robust strategy that aligns with business goals.
- Build a multidisciplinary team with diverse expertise.
- Make thoughtful initial investments in hardware, software, and training.
- Conduct a thorough risk assessment to address ethical and regulatory challenges.
- Start with pilot projects to gather practical insights and fine-tune your approach.

From Blueprint to Reality: Implementation and Scaling

Building on the foundation laid in Chapter 7.1, the next critical phase in an organization's transformation is implementation. As we've often emphasized, moving from strategy to execution is a complex process fraught with challenges and opportunities.

Data Management: The Lifeblood of AI and Quantum Computing

Data is the cornerstone of any AI or quantum computing initiative. Organizations need to ensure that they have access to high-quality, relevant data. This involves creating a robust data pipeline, ensuring data privacy compliance, and implementing data governance frameworks.

Case Study: Netflix's Data-Driven Recommendation Engine

Netflix's recommendation engine is a prime example of effective data management. By analyzing viewing habits, search queries, and even pause and rewind actions, the engine offers personalized recommendations, contributing to customer engagement and retention.

Workflow Integration: Seamless or Disruptive?

Once the data pipeline is established, the next step is integrating AI and quantum computing solutions into existing workflows. This can be a seamless process with proper planning but can be disruptive if not carefully managed.

Example: Salesforce's Einstein AI

Salesforce's Einstein AI is designed to integrate seamlessly into the company's existing CRM solutions, offering predictive analytics and automation features that enhance, rather than disrupt, existing workflows.

Scaling: A Balancing Act

As pilot projects prove successful, the next challenge is scaling these technologies across the organization. This involves hardware and software upgrades, training programs, and possibly organizational restructuring.

Example: Amazon's Use of Robotics in Warehousing

Amazon started with robotics in a few warehouses and has now scaled it across most of its fulfillment centers. The company invested in both hardware and employee training to make this transition smooth.

Ongoing Optimization: The Path of Continuous Improvement

AI and quantum computing technologies are not "set it and forget it" solutions. They require ongoing optimization to adapt to changing conditions, whether it's market dynamics, data variability, or technological advancements.

Case Study: Google's Continuous Algorithm Updates

Google is known for continually optimizing its search algorithms, taking into account user behavior, website quality, and several other factors. This ongoing optimization ensures that the search engine remains accurate and relevant.

Ethical and Regulatory Compliance: An Ongoing Commitment

As organizations move from pilot projects to full-scale implementation, ethical and regulatory compliance becomes even more critical. The scale at which data is collected and analyzed increases, and so does the potential for ethical missteps.

Example: IBM's Commitment to Ethical AI

IBM has set up an internal AI Ethics Board that reviews all its AI projects for ethical considerations. They have also published their ethical guidelines, setting a precedent for other organizations.

Challenges and Pitfalls: Navigating the Rough Waters

Every transformative journey comes with its share of challenges and pitfalls, from technological hurdles like data silos and integration issues to human factors like resistance to change.

Case Study: U.S. Department of Defense's Project Maven

The U.S. Department of Defense's Project Maven aimed to implement AI in military drone footage analysis. However, it faced significant internal resistance, leading to a scaling back of the project.

The path from blueprint to reality is long and fraught with challenges, but with careful planning, execution, and ongoing optimization, organizations can harness the transformative power of AI and quantum computing.

Key Takeaways

- Robust data management is crucial for the success of AI and quantum computing initiatives.
- Seamless workflow integration is essential for minimizing disruption.
- Scaling requires a balanced approach, considering technological and human factors.
- Ongoing optimization ensures that the implemented solutions continue to deliver value.
- Ethical and regulatory compliance is not a one-time activity but an ongoing commitment.

Fostering a Culture of Innovation: The Bedrock of Sustainable Transformation

Technological transformation isn't just about integrating new tools or adopting cutting-edge algorithms. As we've often emphasized, it's equally about fostering a culture that embraces change and innovation. This culture serves as the bedrock for sustainable transformation.

Leadership: The Guiding Light

Leadership plays a critical role in shaping the culture of an organization. Leaders must not only be visionary but also capable of inspiring their teams to embrace change. They should be able to articulate a clear roadmap for integrating AI and quantum computing into the organization's core functions.

Case Study: Satya Nadella at Microsoft

Under Satya Nadella's leadership, Microsoft has undergone a remarkable transformation, pivoting towards cloud computing and AI. Nadella's leadership style has been one of inclusion, open dialogue, and continual learning, which has fostered a culture of innovation at Microsoft.

Employee Engagement: The Human Element

Employees are the foot soldiers in any transformation journey. They must be trained not just in new technologies but also in new ways of thinking. Employee engagement programs, hackathons, and continuous learning modules can help in keeping the workforce aligned with the organization's innovation goals.

Example: Adobe's Kickbox Program
Adobe's Kickbox program provides employees with resources and freedom to work on their own innovative projects, thereby fostering a culture of internal entrepreneurship and continual learning.

Ethical Considerations: The Moral Compass

As organizations delve deeper into AI and quantum computing, ethical considerations take center stage. A culture that prioritizes ethical considerations is more likely to implement these technologies in a responsible manner.

Example: Salesforce's Office of Ethical and Humane Use
Salesforce has set up an Office of Ethical and Humane Use of Technology to ensure that its AI and other techno-

logical initiatives align with ethical principles, setting an industry standard.

Long-Term Sustainability: Beyond the Hype

For innovation to be sustainable, it must go beyond the initial hype and become ingrained in the organization's DNA. This involves long-term planning, investment in R&D, and a commitment to continually reassess and adapt the innovation strategy.

> **Case Study: Apple's Long-Term Focus on User Experience**
>
> *Apple's long-term commitment to innovation is evident in its focus on user experience and design thinking. Despite the changing technological landscape, this core focus has allowed Apple to sustain its position as an industry leader.*

Innovation is as much about culture as it is about technology. Organizations that foster a culture of continuous learning, ethical considerations, and long-term thinking are better positioned to leverage the transformative potential of AI and quantum computing.

Key Takeaways

- Leadership sets the tone for an organization's culture of innovation.
- Employee engagement is crucial for the human element in technological transformation.
- Ethical considerations must be integral to an organization's

innovation culture.
- Long-term sustainability requires going beyond the hype to make innovation a core part of the organizational DNA.

Chapter 8: Summary and Future Outlook

Artificial Intelligence and Quantum Computing: Pioneers of the Smart Age

We are in the midst of a transformative era that we've termed the "Smart Age," characterized by unprecedented advancements in AI and quantum computing. These technologies are not isolated phenomena; they are deeply interwoven into the fabric of various sectors, including healthcare, education, retail, and government.

The Spectrum of Applications

From personalized learning and advanced diagnostics to secure national networks and efficient public services, AI and quantum computing have a wide range of applications that can revolutionize existing systems and create new opportunities.

Ethical and Regulatory Challenges

As these technologies become more pervasive, ethical and regulatory challenges such as data privacy, algorithmic bias, and workforce adaptation are becoming increasingly important.

Balancing technological innovation with ethical responsibility is paramount.

Future Outlook and What to Expect in the Coming Years

In the coming years, expect to see an accelerated adoption of AI and quantum computing technologies across sectors. Companies and governments that are early adopters are likely to gain a competitive edge.

Technological advancements in machine learning algorithms, quantum-resistant cryptography, and data analytics will continue to evolve, offering more robust and efficient solutions for complex problems.

As the technologies mature, we can anticipate a new set of regulations aimed at ensuring responsible use. Organizations must be agile in adapting to these regulatory changes.

The integration of these technologies will necessitate a new skill set from the workforce. Upskilling and reskilling will be essential for adapting to the new technological landscape.

Final Remarks

We stand on the cusp of a new era, one that holds immense promise but also presents complex challenges. As we've often emphasized, including in our presentations , publications as well as in this book, navigating this landscape will require not just technological innovation but also ethical and social considerations.

Organizations and sectors willing to embrace these technologies responsibly are likely to thrive in this new era, marking a significant milestone in human progress. However, the path ahead is not without its hurdles, and it will require collective effort—across sectors, disciplines, and borders—to navigate it successfully.

By understanding the transformative potential and challenges of AI and quantum computing, we can better prepare for a future that promises to be as complex as it is exciting.

Smart Machines demand Smart Choices

ABOUT

This morning you woke up in the "Smart Machine Age" , encapsulated in the time we find ourselves in, characterized by unprecedented advancements in technology. Unlike any other period in human history, this era is driven by intelligent machines that can learn, adapt, and even make decisions. We've moved beyond the simple digitization of tasks to a realm where machines can analyze vast amounts of data, make complex calculations in nanoseconds, and automate decision-making processes that would take humans considerably longer. AI and Quantum will have a enormous impact on business , society and people. Emerging trends are often overrated on the short term but underestimated on the long run. Follow me in the world of emerging technologies and explore how AI and Quantum can transform the world.

www.ingramcontent.com/pod-product-compliance
Lightning Source LLC
Chambersburg PA
CBHW060956260726
48661CB00005B/1896